THE CHILTERN MURDER STORIES

RECALLING THE EVENTS OF SOME OF THE MOST
WELL-KNOWN MURDERS IN THE CHILTERNS

Neil Walden

BRADWELL
BOOKS

Published by Bradwell Books

9 Orgreave Close Sheffield S13 9NP

Email: books@bradwellbooks.co.uk

British Library Cataloguing in Publication Data: a catalogue record for this book is available from the British Library.

1st Edition

ISBN: 9781910551974

Print: Gomer Press, Llandysul, Ceredigion SA44 4JL

Artwork by: Andrew Caffrey

Photograph Credits: The author and indicated separately

CONTENTS

INTRODUCTION

All of the true murder stories to be found in this book come from the Chilterns area of England. They are spread between the relevant parts of Buckinghamshire, Oxfordshire, Hertfordshire and Bedfordshire.

Chronologically speaking, the first story told is from 1822 concerning a murder at a toll house in Aston Clinton. The book then covers the next 120 years and finishes with what may be the most famous case of them all: the Luton sack murder.

The sixteen murder cases related in these pages resulted in nineteen deaths. There are two shootings, three stabbings and a poisoning. The remainder were brutally beaten to death in some way or another. As all the stories come from a time when the death penalty was still in place it is not surprising that eight of the murderers went to the scaffold. Three of the cases still remain unsolved.

While the title of each of the chapters is taken from contemporary newspaper reports of the crimes, I have not used any pictures of crime scenes at the time of the murders themselves. In each case I have attempted to leave this to the imagination and instead I have opted to show sites and scenes which are important to each case and that are still visible today.

THE MURDER OF SARAH HART

ONE OF THE MOST FAMOUS MURDER STORIES OF ALL TIME IS THAT CONCERNING DR CRIPPEN. IN 1910 HE BECAME THE FIRST SUSPECT TO BE CAPTURED WITH THE AID OF WIRELESS TELEGRAPHY. LESS WELL KNOWN IS THE FACT THAT THE FIRST MURDERER TO BE CAUGHT THROUGH THE USE OF ANY SORT OF TELECOMMUNICATIONS WAS BACK IN 1845, WHEN THE NEW TECHNOLOGY WAS USED TO CATCH THE BERKHAMSTED MURDERER, JOHN TAWELL.

The family of John Tawell were from Norfolk and his illustrious ancestors even included a mayor of Norwich. His father was a shopkeeper near Beccles and in his youth John Tawell worked in this shop, as well as a series of others in the East Anglia region. Many of the places where Tawell worked were owned by people from the Quaker community and it was through those connections that he learned of their beliefs, something which was to prove very useful in later life as he sought to conceal his criminal activities.

It is in 1814, when Tawell was already 30 years of age, that he first comes to our attention for attempting to forge a

£10 note. At this time forgery was a capital offence and at his trial he was sentenced to death. Fortunately for him, and largely due to the compassionate nature of the company which he had attempted to defraud, the sentence was commuted to transportation to Australia for 14 years.

While in exile, Tawell managed to impress many people with his medical knowledge which had been picked up when working for a London chemist's shop. Soon Tawell was working in a rudimentary convict hospital and his employers were sufficiently impressed to start the process of attempting to gain him a pardon.

Once he was again a free man, and despite his total lack of any appropriate qualifications, Tawell soon set up a chemist's shop of his own. While the shop, based in Sydney, was extremely successful this was not the limit of his ambitions. The money that Tawell accumulated was soon invested in property and later an export business. By the mid-1820s Tawell was a wealthy man and had been joined in Australia by his family from England. On the surface the ex-convict was a pillar of the Quaker community and able to fund the first Friends Meeting House in Sydney.

In 1831 Tawell and his family returned to London. When

Tawell became a widower in 1838 he soon began an affair with the nurse who had attended his wife through her final illness. This nurse was called Sarah Hart and the couple remained together for quite some time, having two children together. By 1841 Tawell was also keeping the company of a Quaker schoolmistress. In the February of that year Tawell married his new love and was living in Berkhamsted while Sarah was moved out of harm's way to a cottage outside Slough.

To start with Tawell paid for the cottage and also provided some money towards Sarah's upkeep. But at about this time his various business interests began to falter. With Tawell no longer in Australia to look after the businesses himself, they started to experience financial difficulties and he looked around to see where economies could be made. Suddenly Sarah's position had become very vulnerable.

On 1st January 1845, Tawell went to a chemist in Bishopsgate Street in London where he purchased two bottles of 'Steele's Acid'. This was known as a treatment for varicose veins and contained poisonous prussic acid. Back in Slough, one of her near neighbours saw Tawell leaving Sarah's house and not long afterwards could hear Sarah moaning with pain, having drunk some beer which had been laced with poison. It was clear to those anxious to help the dying Sarah that Tawell must surely be responsible in some way. The local vicar, who was one of the first to see the stricken Sarah, followed Tawell to the station in the hope of intercepting him. While he was too late to stop the escape, he did witness Tawell boarding the train for London.

The vicar spoke with the stationmaster, hoping that the train could be stopped or intercepted in some way, and it was at this point that Tawell's pursuers turned to the new technology. The electric telegraph was used to send a message from Slough station to Paddington. The pertinent information it contained was that Tawell was on the 7.42 train and dressed in his distinctive Quaker outfit.

The duty Sergeant at Paddington was alerted to the imminent arrival of the murderer and he arranged to be there to meet the train. In fact there was not the satisfaction of an immediate arrest. One assumes that there was a certain suspicion about the new technology and that further corroboration was needed. Instead, the police followed Tawell, who seemed to have little in the way of a guilty conscience as he went about his business in a fairly ordinary way, buying some sweets and stopping for a cup of coffee. Finally, Tawell went to his lodgings just off Cornhill in the City of London and, having seen that he was settled for the night, the police returned to Paddington.

The following morning, when they came to arrest him, Tawell had already left his lodgings. Fortunately for them he was still blissfully unaware that he was the prime suspect in the murder case and he had nonchalantly gone back to the Jerusalem Coffee House where he was now arrested.

The trial of John Tawell opened at Aylesbury County Court on 12th March 1845 and the prisoner was to plead not guilty. The courthouse was only able to hold a fraction of the people from the surrounding villages who were desperate to see Tawell tried for his life.

Cowper's Court,
a small alley just off
Cornhill in the City of
London and the site of
the Jerusalem Coffee
House where Tawell
was arrested
The Author

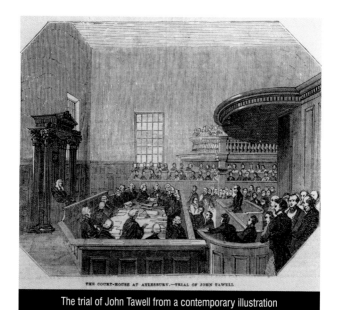

THE COURT-HOUSE AT AYLESBURY.—TRIAL OF JOHN TAWELL

The trial of John Tawell from a contemporary illustration

Among those attending the trial was Tawell's own five-year-old son from his relationship with Sarah.

The defence had more than a hint of desperation about it, largely claiming that Sarah's death had been caused by eating apple pips. The argument was that prussic acid occurred naturally in the pips and that Sarah's death was surely caused by her eating a huge amount of fruit. The argument was not terribly compelling and, for the second time in his life, Tawell was found guilty and handed a death sentence.

Once more there was to be a plea for clemency. Despite the disservice that Tawell's behaviour had done them, the Quakers petitioned the Crown in the hope of having the sentence commuted to life imprisonment. The argument was that no one really knew what had happened in the house itself on the day of Sarah's death and perhaps she had willingly taken the poison. It was a pretty hopeless case and the death sentence remained in place.

Tawell now made a full confession. He claimed that his motive had been fear of Sarah's existence coming to the attention of his new wife. However, this is unlikely to be the whole story. A friend of Tawell's later related an earlier incident where a letter from Sarah had already been discovered by the new Mrs Tawell in one of John's pockets. It was a letter in which Sarah asked for money as John had not paid her anything for the children for some time. It seems that the contents of the letter, indicating that Sarah had become a financial drain on his resources, rather than the discovery of the letter itself, was Tawell's main motive.

At 8am on Friday 28th March 1845 John Tawell was publicly hanged in Aylesbury. Contemporary reports say that more than 10,000 people attended this grisly event.

THE HENLEY MURDER

LAMBRIDGE HOUSE NEAR HENLEY WAS OWNED BY A LONDON SHOPKEEPER AND, WHENEVER HE AND HIS FAMILY WERE AWAY, IT WAS LOOKED AFTER BY A MISS KATE DUNGEY. ON THE EVENING OF 8TH DECEMBER 1893 KATE WAS MURDERED. THE CASE REMAINS UNSOLVED AND IT IS ONE OF THE ABIDING MYSTERIES OF THE CHILTERNS AREA.

Leasing the house at the time of Kate's murder was a man called Henry Mash. He was a fruiterer with his business based in Charing Cross Road. The company was well known in the Chilterns and elsewhere and at one point was based in Chesham.

Kate was 29 years old and from Goudhurst in Kent and she had worked for the Mash family for seven years, initially as a nursery governess to his children and subsequently as a housekeeper. Mr Mash and his family were frequently away at their main residence at Redcliffe Gardens in a fashionable part of London and Kate would be left in charge. The Lambridge estate also included a small farm run by George Dawson and employing two young boys who would sleep up at the big house in order to keep Kate company.

At about 8.30 pm on 8th December the boys returned to Lambridge after an evening out and, despite knowing that Kate was in the house, found that the doors were locked and that they were unable to get back in. They roused George Dawson to see if he could help them get into the house. When all three of them returned from Dawson's farm they found that the guard dog, who lived outside, was extremely dopey and that the bay window was now swinging open, something that had not been the case when the boys had visited a little earlier.

With great trepidation the search party entered through the open doors. Although the house was found to be empty, there were bloodstains to be seen. There was no sign of Kate in the house but, when they widened their search to the garden and grounds, they found Kate's body on the edge of the nearby wood, about thirty yards from the house. It seems that she had been killed by a series of blows to the head. Nearby there was a poker, but it was thought unlikely that this was the murder weapon, and more probable that Kate had taken it in an attempt to defend herself.

The police were summoned from Henley and the story was pieced together. Closer inspection of the house revealed that a tussle had taken place in the hall. It seemed that it was here that Kate had been attacked and that she had attempted to get away from the intruder. After compiling that summary of events, rather incredibly, the police called it a day and went home for the night. The keys to the house were put in the hands of the ever-helpful George Dawson. Not a great move from the scene of crime officers as surely, at this early stage, George would have been one of the main suspects.

When investigations resumed the next morning, an examination of Kate's body suggested that she had died in the early evening, but possibly as late as 8 pm. If it was at the latter end of that timescale, then it does seem possible that the murderer was in the house when the boys first returned home. The murderer must then have fled through the window during the period that they had been away getting help.

Unlikely as it seemed, the motive for the attack began to look as though it was some sort of personal grudge. It could have been a robbery that went wrong, but the Mash family were now summoned to Lambridge and found that nothing was missing. Interestingly, Kate's pockets had been turned inside out as if something specific had been searched for.

If the purpose of the attack was simply to murder Kate, then it made little sense. Kate herself had few enemies, although she had disagreed with Dawson in the past about a number of topics, albeit that they were fairly insignificant in nature. However, there was a feeling that the murderer was well acquainted with the farm.

And now there was an arrest. It was Walter Rathall, who was Dawson's brother-in-law, a 23-year-old native of Henley and former farmworker who had recently returned to the area. It was said that Rathall had received an unexpected inheritance from his mother, who everyone had assumed to be poor, and he had then disappeared from Lambridge on a spending spree. Rathall was known to have once quarrelled with Kate during his time there. The main disagreement had been that Kate had lent him some money when they were on better terms and he had failed to pay her back.

Rathall's behaviour could not have been more conspicuous as he went around the area leaving debts and using improbable aliases. It is also said that he was heard to be taunting the police. Rathall was brought back to Henley police station for questioning. He produced alibis for most of the period of the past few weeks, but there was a noticeable exception as he was unable to produce a credible alibi for the exact time period in which, in all probability, Kate had been murdered.

Following Rathall's arrest more than one paper claimed to have found the key to the story, which they said was that over the last four years Kate had been involved with a married man in nearby Assendon. More recently, the wife of this mystery man had become aware of Kate's existence and there had been a huge argument. It was confidently asserted that this husband and wife would be giving evidence at the trial. But there was to be no trial and the simple truth is that there was no compelling evidence to support this theory. Kate was not involved in a love affair as far as anyone knew.

Rathall was never sent to trial for the murder. There were footprints in the mud at the scene of the crime which showed some similarities to Rathall's boots, but there was some bickering as to whether it was a true match or not. It also seemed that Kate had made a very spirited attempt to defend herself and yet Rathall had no signs of being in a fight, and none of his clothing had shown any signs of blood splatters.

Had the murder even been the work of just one man? The attack showed that there had been two weapons used, and possibly there had been two assailants. Then there is the part played by George Dawson in all of this. Dawson seemed to have found Kate's body with remarkable ease, something that his fellow searchers had remarked upon. Did he know more than he was admitting?

Many speculated that there were certain aspects of the case that indicated that the murderer was a woman. Perhaps if it was a woman (maybe even a woman who was related to the family in some way) she would have had fewer qualms about murdering the housekeeper, but not the family's much-loved black retriever, who was merely sedated.

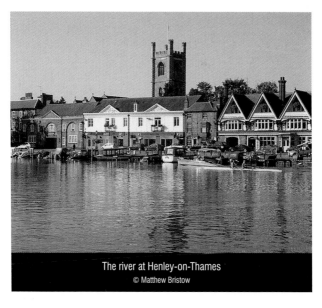

The river at Henley-on-Thames
© Matthew Bristow

One day the previous summer Kate had been seen crying and she related a story to Dawson about how Mrs Mash was going to hit her with an umbrella, and she would have done so had Mr Mash not intervened. Mr Mash's wife, Georgiana, was a year older than her husband and was originally from Sussex. There is nothing to suggest that it was not a happy marriage and when Henry Mash died in 1919 they had been married for fifty years. While it would be wrong to think she had any involvement in the murder, it certainly would have been good to know more about this umbrella incident, but it was dismissed as being irrelevant to the case at the inquest.

The Henley Murder has never been solved.

THE WIFE MURDER AT DUNSTABLE

DAVID AND ELIZA DUMPLETON LIVED IN ST MARY'S STREET, IN WHAT HAS NOW BECOME THE MUCH-REDEVELOPED PART OF DUNSTABLE NEAR TO ST MARY'S GATE. BY JANUARY 1876 THE COUPLE HAD BEEN MARRIED FOR EIGHT YEARS AND HAD NO CHILDREN. THE RELATIONSHIP WAS STRAINED AS IT SEEMS THAT DAVID BELIEVED THAT ELIZA HAD BEEN UNFAITHFUL TO HIM. THE NEXT-DOOR NEIGHBOUR WAS A FRIEND CALLED JOSEPH BUNKER AND IT WAS HE WHO CALLED THE POLICE WHEN DAVID CALMLY ANNOUNCED, *'I BELIEVE I HAVE KILLED THE MISSUS.'*

In view of the difficult relationship between the Dumpletons, David's admission certainly seemed plausible and Bunker hurried up Middle Row in the hope of finding a policeman. Outside the Red Lion hotel, which stood on the corner of High Street North and Church Street, Bunker bumped into Sergeant Addington and PC Totfield. Bunker explained the situation and all three of them quickly returned to the Dumpletons' house.

With a flicker of life found to be left in Eliza, Dr Farr was summoned (by coincidence he was also David's employer, where he worked as a groom) and Eliza was moved from the floor to the sofa in the front room. Eliza lived on for a further 15 minutes before breathing her last. She had been struck on the head and stabbed three times in the throat and forehead.

David never made any attempt to get away and now, with him under arrest, a search was made of the house. As there had never been much doubt of his guilt it seems strange that Dumpleton should have hidden the weapons used in the attack, and yet this was the case as a knife and a coal hammer were retrieved from the cellar. The police noted that two human hairs were visible on the hammer, but were later unable to produce this valuable evidence in court as apparently they blew away in a gust of wind as they went back outside. Fortunately that kind of evidence was not critical as David was clearly guilty.

In the immediate wake of the murder there was an uncomfortable sense that people actually believed that at some level Eliza was only getting what she deserved. As if in justification of her husband's actions, there were even reports about how Eliza had failed to make his tea. But as time went on public opinion began to swing back in favour of Eliza. Soon letters appeared in the newspaper in support of her. A previous employer attested to Eliza's good character and happy demeanour, saying that the only time that she ever seemed miserable was at the mention of her husband's name. Two hundred people attended her funeral and it was at this time that a rumour circulated that David, overcome with the remorse that was so lacking at the time of his arrest, had killed himself in Bedford Gaol while awaiting his trial. In fact David Dumpleton was alive and well.

At the inquest into the death of Eliza Dumpleton the coroner was adamant that David should be tried for murder rather than manslaughter. His reasoning was that had the death resulted from just the attack with the coal hammer then manslaughter would probably be the correct charge, but Dumpleton had changed his weapon to a knife in order to complete the assault and therefore had not acted in the heat of the moment. Nevertheless, the jury at the inquest would not take guidance from the coroner and returned a verdict of death by manslaughter. It was this lesser charge that Dumpleton was to face in court. The large crowd appeared to be delighted by this outcome and cheered wildly.

At the end of his trial on 7th March 1876 David Dumpleton was duly found guilty of manslaughter and sentenced to twelve years' penal servitude. His prison records indicate that this was served in Pentonville and at Chatham Prison in Kent. Nine years into his sentence Dumpleton was released on licence and he returned to the Chilterns area. He died in St. Albans at the age of 51 on 23rd April 1895.

David Dumpleton at the time of his arrest
© Bill Walden

THE HEMEL HEMPSTEAD CANAL MURDER

HENRY, JOHN AND JAMES BERRY WERE THE CREW OF THE CANAL BOAT THE BETSY. ALL THREE OF THEM WERE ON BOARD ON THE NIGHT OF SATURDAY 11TH JUNE 1836 WHEN THE BOAT MOORED UP FOR THE EVENING ON THE GRAND JUNCTION CANAL CLOSE TO BOXMOOR IN HEMEL HEMPSTEAD. BY THE NEXT MORNING THEY WOULD BE INVOLVED IN A FIGHT THAT WOULD RESULT IN THE DEATH OF ONE OF THE THREE BROTHERS.

The Berry brothers were from Eynsham, about five miles north-west of Oxford. At this time they were working for a customer, Mr Henry Ward, who was a coal merchant from Oxford, although it seems that they were actually employed by a businessman called Mr Heron.

At two o'clock on that Sunday morning in June, James woke and then roused Henry believing that the Betsy, where they were sleeping, had been cut loose from its moorings. On inspection, not only did this prove to be the case, but they also found that a cupboard at the stern of the boat had been opened and searched. Some things, although fairly trivial, had been stolen. The missing items included crockery, candles and a small amount of food.

Looking to the shore, the brothers could see a house about sixty yards away which, despite the early hour, had its lights blazing. They could also see three men who, on realising they had been spotted, guiltily retreated into the house. This was the home of one of the three men, who was called Goodwin Hall. The other two men were James Baldwin and John Hall and all three of them were local labourers.

James and Henry re-moored the Betsy and watched the house from a distance. Initially they could not be certain that Goodwin Hall and his two friends had been responsible for the robbery, but soon the situation was to escalate alarmingly.

Within half an hour the same three men, this time accompanied by two women, left the house and approached the boat once more. Their intentions at this stage were not entirely clear but when they were within a few yards of the boat James Berry challenged them, saying that the boat had been robbed and he wanted to know if they were responsible. The group were angered by the accusation, and there followed a big argument. Goodwin Hall threatened to come on board to sort James out and in return James said that if did set foot on the Betsy he would shoot him. With the quarrel becoming more serious the Berry brothers duly got their gun, while Baldwin jumped on board and one of the women went to go and get Goodwin Hall's rifle from the house.

The Fishery Lock on the Grand Union Canal close to where the Betsy moored on the night of the murder © Mr Biz

James Berry was knocked to the ground by Baldwin and he tumbled down below into the cabin. One of the assailants now threw a rock which struck James on the head with a terrible blow. Goodwin Hall was also on board the boat by this time and, from the evidence presented at the trial, it seems likely that it was he who was responsible for throwing the rock. Certainly from Henry Berry's description of the attack Goodwin Hall would have been in the ideal position, above the cabin, to make the attack.

At this point, with James Berry virtually unconscious, Baldwin realised that things had escalated out of control. He wanted to call it a day and shake hands with the crew of the Betsy and part as friends but it had all gone way too far for that. Realising that they were in serious trouble, Goodwin Hall and the gang returned to the house while Henry and John tried to attend to the terrible head wound that their brother had received in the fight. With it being the early hours of the morning they were unable to get any help nearby and so they made their way on to Uxbridge in the barge. When a doctor was found the true severity of the wound was established and the remaining two brothers were told that James would probably not live.

James Berry was now taken back to Oxford by coach where he was soon examined at the Radcliffe Infirmary. On the Thursday after the attack an operation was carried out on Berry's fractured skull but it was too late to save him and he died the following evening.

The labourers were arrested and were sent to trial. It soon became clear that there was no real case against John Hall, the third member of the gang, as he did not actually board the Betsy. However, the case against Goodwin Hall and Baldwin was fairly straightforward. The defence was that Berry had in fact struck his head on the side of the boat as he tumbled down the stairs, but there was little doubt that they were going to be found guilty.

The verdict was that Berry's death was not wilful murder, but rather that it was manslaughter. A sentence of transportation for life was passed. Clearly the convicts' previous criminal records, which were littered with cases of poaching, thieving and assaults, were taken into account and acted against them, the recommendation being that the prisoners should be transported to 'The Worst Country' – which would mean Australia.

The prisoners were held in a prison hulk in Chatham for some months. And then, six months after their boarding of the Betsy, the two convicts climbed aboard another vessel, this time the prison ship the *Prince George,* bound for New South Wales.

THE LONELY INN MURDER

SARAH BLAKE RAN THE CROWN AND ANCHOR AT GALLOWSTREE COMMON, ABOUT FIVE MILES NORTH OF READING. HER NEIGHBOUR, MRS PAYNE CAME ROUND TO SEE HER ON 4TH MARCH 1922. THERE WAS NO RESPONSE AND SO SHE FORCED AN ENTRY AND SOON FOUND MRS BLAKE DEAD IN A POOL OF BLOOD IN THE KITCHEN. HER SKULL WAS FRACTURED AND SHE HAD RECEIVED MULTIPLE WOUNDS IN DEFENDING HERSELF. THERE WAS NO EVIDENCE OF MONEY BEING MISSING AND THE CRIME SEEMED TO HAVE NO MOTIVE.

Sarah had last been seen on 3rd March in the early part of the evening and it was deduced that she had been murdered shortly after that sighting. There were clues to be found as the murderer had left bloody fingerprints here and there and, most oddly of all, had the time and confidence to stay on and pour himself a drink after the murder. The impression was that the intruder seemed to know his way around the various rooms and was familiar with the premises.

The Reformation, where Hewitt went to collect beer on the night of the murder © Colin Bates

Two people had been in the Crown and Anchor that evening, one of whom swiftly became the prime suspect. He was a fifteen-year-old named Jack Hewitt. The young boy was questioned but the investigation of Hewitt was swiftly adjourned when Robert Alfred Sheppard, a 22-year-old wood-chopper from Reading, was arrested for an unrelated burglary and promptly and voluntarily admitted involvement in the murder of Mrs Blake.

Sheppard's initial story was that he was the lookout

for the gang that carried out the crime, but soon he was saying that he had committed the murder alone. Sheppard's behaviour was complicated and contradictory as he seemed to be weighing up which of his crimes would be treated most leniently as he wove the various stories together to come up with a new version of events. He claimed at one point to have travelled to the pub on a stolen bicycle, where he met up with a chap called Jack Larkin, who was the real culprit. By the time that Sheppard was up before the magistrate in Reading police court a few days later he was disowning the confession and saying that it had been obtained under duress.

By now a knife had been found in a hedge about 35 yards from the door of the pub. This was covered in blood and had human hair on the blade. Initially the knife was thought to be Sheppard's, but it was now identified as belonging to Hewitt, the initial suspect. When he was questioned again it was now Hewitt's turn to make a full confession. He claimed that it was simply a motiveless crime and that once he had been alone with Mrs Blake in the early evening he had struck her with an iron bar in a frenzied attack. He is recorded as saying, *'I wish I had never seen the pictures, they are the cause of this,'* intimating that scenes which he had seen at the cinema had driven him to commit the crime. Surely there are few films of that vintage which would show the type of violence that had been exhibited in the frenzied attack on a defenceless old woman.

At his trial at the Oxford Assizes in June 1922 Hewitt pleaded not guilty. He now claimed that bloodstains found on his clothes were from killing rabbits and the knife was not his. Hewitt's account of his movements on the night of the murder was that he had been to the Crown and Anchor, but had then come home to his mother who sent him back out to buy some beer from the same pub. Finding it to be inexplicably shut, he now went to an alternative pub around the corner in order to complete the errand.

Hewitt made a particularly poor impression in the dock as he failed to account for how he acquired and then disposed of the knife. At times he claimed to have lent it and sold it, before finally claiming that he had simply lost it. More believable than the knife stories was his account of how he signed his confession without fully understanding it. It seems possible that Hewitt could have been pressurised in some way into signing a confession that he did not understand. Certainly there were protests at the trial at Oxford Assizes that some of the evidence was inadmissible due to the failure of the police to caution Hewitt correctly.

In the end, the right verdict was reached although there are a few puzzling aspects to the case. There was still no sign of the iron bar that had been used in the attack and there was talk of a cyclist who was seen coming up to the door of the pub but was never traced, unless this was Sheppard on the stolen bicycle.

The jury found Hewitt guilty but because of his youth, he was spared the gallows and was sentenced to be detained indefinitely at His Majesty's pleasure.

Robert Sheppard, however, continued his life of crime. As soon as the prosecution offered no evidence against him he was discharged, only to be instantly re-arrested for the offence of the burglary committed at about the time of Sarah's murder. Sheppard received a sentence of six months in prison. On release he moved to Drayton Road in Tottenham to live with Florence Jones, a young cook he had met when she was working in Henley. In the September of 1923 he was tried for the murder of Florence, found guilty and sentenced to death. This time his defence was that the killing was a suicide pact that had gone wrong. The execution was scheduled for 9th November 1923 but Sheppard escaped the gallows when the sentence was commuted to life imprisonment.

THE DOUBLE MURDER AT PITSTONE

ON THE EVENING OF 12TH DECEMBER 1891 TWO GAMEKEEPERS NAMED WILLIAM PUDDEPHATT AND JOSEPH CRAWLEY SET OFF TO PATROL THE WOODS KNOWN AS ALDBURY NOWERS, CLOSE TO TRING IN HERTFORDSHIRE. ON THIS OCCASION NEITHER OF THE TWO MEN WERE ARMED. IT WAS TO BE THE LAST TIME THAT THEY WERE SEEN ALIVE. AT ELEVEN O'CLOCK THE FOLLOWING DAY THEIR BODIES WERE DISCOVERED IN A NEARBY PLOUGHED FIELD.

The gamekeepers were two members of a team of three who were employed to protect the hunting rights of the estate. When they failed to return, several local men went looking for them and it was not long before they came across the body of 42-year-old Joseph Crawley. He had suffered severe blows to the back of his head. The first impression was that the injuries had been inflicted with a gun, in a beating of such ferocity that it had actually broken the gun apart so that fragments of it could clearly be seen nearby.

The body of 37-year-old William Puddephatt was about 100 yards away. He was lying on his back and it was clear to see that he also had received severe injuries to his head. The small search party now split up. The police in Tring were informed as well as the local doctor and the bodies of the two murdered men were conveyed on carts to the Greyhound pub in Aldbury to await an inquest.

Inevitably the first suspects were always likely to be those known to indulge in poaching. The spotlight fell on two well-known poachers, Frederick Eggleton and a friend of his called Charles Rayner. Eggleton was a labourer aged 35. Rayner was supposedly a chair-turner by trade although he had been a military man for most of his adult life. Now 31 years of age, he had spent 12 years in The King's Shropshire Light Infantry. On the night of the murder these two men, along with another local man named Walter Smith, had been seen out on a pub crawl. They had been spotted in the nearby pub, the Greyhound, where they had something to eat and had even spoken to Puddephatt who was also there prior to starting his evening's work.

While Smith was quickly arrested, there was no sign of the two seasoned poachers. Eggleton and Rayner had gone on the run. When Smith was questioned he claimed to know nothing of the murder and that his next stop after leaving the Greyhound had been back home to bed.

The Double MURDER at Pitstone

A reward of £100 was put on the heads of Eggleton and Rayner. After being spotted in nearby Tring, and then again near Wendover, where the two fugitives were seen 'acting in a furtive manner', they were finally spotted by the police 25 miles south near Slough. At the time that they were apprehended the two suspects were in the company of a shopkeeper called Mr Jennings.

The initial explanation of the two suspects for their flight was that they had simply seen news of the murders in the newspapers, and realising that the descriptions of the wanted men matched their own they had fled in panic. Smith, now knowing that his two friends were in custody in Aylesbury Prison, started to become a little more communicative. He admitted that he had been there on the night of the murder, and that a gun used by the men had been thrown into the nearby canal. The gun was promptly recovered by police. Smith never denied his part in the poaching and the initial skirmish but was now saying that he had left before the fight escalated and insisting that the two game keepers were alive at the time he last saw them.

The trial of the three men took place on 23rd February 1892 at Buckinghamshire Assizes in Aylesbury. All three men admitted being in the woods for the purpose of poaching, but claimed that they had been attacked by Puddephatt and Crawley. Eggleton and Rayner were found guilty of murder and sentenced to death. Smith was found guilty of manslaughter and given twenty years' penal servitude. The execution date was set for Tuesday 17th March.

Public sympathy now began to shift towards the poachers and pleas for leniency appeared in the newspapers: surely the killings happened without premeditation in the heat of the moment and without any witnesses. To the end, Eggleton maintained that he had no recollection of the events as he had been struck on the head, but his belief was that the gamekeepers struck first, and it was he and Rayner who were acting in self-defence. There was no intention to kill anyone.

The Home Secretary came under pressure in the House of Commons to commute the sentence to imprisonment, but he stood firm. The gamekeepers had been brutally murdered and all the evidence suggested that they were struck from behind or even as they lay helpless upon the ground. The execution was duly carried out at Oxford Gaol. Apparently Rayner went to the scaffold wearing his favourite brown deerstalker hat.

The woods still exist and are a haven of peace and tranquillity. Today it is almost impossible to imagine that they were the scene of two gruesome murders.

ATROCIOUS MURDER NEAR AYLESBURY

EARLY IN THE MORNING OF 20TH NOVEMBER 1822 A WORKMAN ON HIS WAY PAST THE TOLL HOUSE AT ASTON CLINTON SAW THAT THE DOOR WAS AJAR. WORRIED FOR THE OWNER'S WELFARE HE TOOK A QUICK LOOK INSIDE AND PROMPTLY FOUND THE BODY OF AN ELDERLY WOMAN LYING ON THE FLOOR. LATER, WHEN HELP HAD BEEN OBTAINED, A FULLER INVESTIGATION OF THE HOUSE REVEALED THAT NOT ONLY HAD THE OWNER RACHEL NEEDLE BEEN MURDERED, BUT ALSO HER HUSBAND, EDWARD, WHOSE BODY WAS FOUND IN THE BEDROOM. BOTH HAD BEEN BEATEN TO DEATH.

Operating from The Kings Arms in Berkhamsted, the authorities attempted to piece together what had happened and track down the murderers. On the evening of the day of the murder the publican of the nearby Bridgewater Arms, a Mr Bennett, reported that there were three new customers in his pub and that they were behaving strangely. Apparently they had bloodstains on their clothes and they had paid for their food and drinks almost entirely in halfpennies, which was surely the coins stolen from the toll house.

When questioned, the alibis of the three suspects did not tally and nor did they seem particularly probable. At least the names that they provided seemed to be genuine enough: they were Martha Barnacle, James Crocker and Thomas Randall. Randall and Crocker flatly denied being involved in the murder in any way but Martha's story certainly allowed for the possibility of the two men being responsible. She talked of them having disappeared together around the time of the murder, claiming that they needed to go out on a mysterious errand of some sort.

At the subsequent inquest into the death of the elderly couple, witnesses were able to recall seeing two men in the vicinity of the toll house who were said to very much resemble Crocker and Randall. They had been spotted again the following morning, this time accompanied by someone who was, in all probability, Martha. Although the evidence was not conclusive, items found on the two men were thought to belong to Mr Needle, and all this proved sufficient for the two men to be committed to trial.

The trial started on 4th March 1823. In the intervening weeks Crocker and Randall had decided on very different plans of action. While Randall maintained his innocence, Crocker now readily admitted his guilt. The judge made sure that Crocker understood the repercussions of his actions as it would certainly mean the death penalty for him, but Crocker insisted that he knew what he was doing and persisted with his plea of guilty

A series of landladies and lodging house owners were able to pinpoint the three suspects as being in the area in the period directly prior to the murder. Evidence was presented which included a pair of shoes that were discovered in the two men's bundles that were recognised as coming from the Needles' house. There was also a pair of gloves that were identified as belonging to Mr Needle. Other possessions of the elderly couple had also been found on them while still more items had been retrieved from a field on the Tring to Berkhamsted road, where they had been hidden.

With Randall and Crocker entering different pleas it made Martha's evidence all the more important. Martha was 26 years of age and from Cubbington in Warwickshire although she travelled widely selling cottons and laces. She was a closer friend of Randall than she was of Crocker, believing that one day she and

Randall would be married. She was less impressed by Crocker, whom she claimed they had met on the road. Martha's account of their motives and movements becomes a little confused at that point, but certainly the three of them discussed prospective trips to London and Oxford. The period around the night of the Needles' murder had found them lodging in Berkhamsted. Martha maintained that she was not with the two men on the night of the murders but that they had met up the following morning and at that point Randall, in particular, seemed anxious to leave the town.

With Crocker silently accepting his guilt and Randall tight-lipped about exactly what had happened on the night of the murder, the two men were found guilty and the judge duly passed the sentence of death on both men.

The feeling up until the executions had been that perhaps Crocker had been the mastermind and that Randall had fallen under his influence. But the truth may not have been that simple. In fact, Crocker had had a series of entirely legitimate jobs and was known to have done well in his career prior to meeting Randall for the first time, which was only a few weeks before the murders were committed. Crocker had been born in Langford Budville in Somerset and had started out as a baker in London. Randall, on the other hand, had pretty much always lived a life of crime. He was now 24 years old and although nothing suggests that he had committed a murder prior to the killings at the toll house, he had certainly been involved in burglary and pickpocketing around his native Warwickshire. Usually Randall used the name of John Bryan and in fact the letters sent from his prison cell still preferred this alias.

The Kings Arms, Berkhamsted where the rudimentary 'incident room' was set up © Anna Kipluks

It seems that Randall and Crocker had gone on something of a crime spree. They were convinced that a toll house would have a decent amount of takings after a day's work and so they attempted the robbery with violence. When the proceeds of the robbery proved to be something of a disappointment they promptly ran out of ideas and attempted the most lacklustre of escape plans.

With just two days left before the execution, Randall became agitated and particularly keen to catch up with Martha. Martha's evidence had done as much as anyone's to seal the fate of Randall and it was initially thought that it might not be the best of ideas for the two of them to meet up once more. Yet, when it was allowed, the meeting was perfectly cordial and Randall seemed completely resigned to his fate.

The two men were executed outside Aylesbury Prison on 6th March 1823.

THE MYSTERIOUS MURDER NEAR LUTON

WHEN WILLIAM BRADBURY LEFT THE OLD ENGLISH GENTLEMAN INN ON THE HITCHIN ROAD IN LUTON JUST BEFORE MIDNIGHT ON 3RD AUGUST 1867, IT WAS THE LAST TIME THAT HE WOULD BE SEEN ALIVE. ABOUT TEN MINUTES LATER HE WAS FOUND DYING IN THE STREET HAVING BEING BLUDGEONED ON THE HEAD WITH A BLUNT INSTRUMENT.

William Bradbury had been an agricultural labourer and one-time gamekeeper who had been born in Lilley in Hertfordshire. Bradbury had just received his wages of 28 shillings. He was now on his way home having spent a fair proportion of his pay on new clothes which he was carrying. These included a pair of trousers, two shirts and a hat.

Drinkers in another pub, The Royal Oak, were alarmed when a man came running in saying that someone had been attacked. Several of the men ran out to lend a hand and found a mortally wounded Bradbury being supported in the arms of a man called William Worsley. Worsley had, it seems, been on a pub crawl that night with two friends, Levi Welch and James Day. In fact it had been Day who had run into the pub to get assistance.

Worsley almost immediately began behaving in a deeply suspicious way. He seemed rather smug and failed miserably to account for why he was there at all. In no time he became the main suspect, although all three men were detained in connection with the murder of Bradbury. Both Worsley and Welch, who were in their mid-forties, were well known to the authorities. Worsley had five convictions and while it was a figure matched by Welch, his were almost exclusively related to breaches of the game laws, as he seemed to be regularly caught poaching. Unlike the other two Day, who at this point was only in his early twenties, was not a habitual criminal and there is no trace of other misdemeanours before or after the murder of William Bradbury. Nevertheless all three were committed to trial on the charge of wilful murder.

Welch was initially unforthcoming about the murder but, realising just how serious the position was, he at last began to explain what had happened on the night of 3rd August. The crucial fact was that it had been Worsley who hit Bradbury with part of the ironwork of a fire grate. By the time of the trial Welch was prepared to accept his guilt for the robbery, for which he was given a term of 14 years' penal servitude. As the trial began all the attention was now on Worsley, whose defence was that he had found the stricken Bradbury on the ground and had simply gone through his pockets to see if there was anything of any value. Welch, now not facing a murder charge, was able to testify against Worsley and the evidence was damning.

The now demolished *Old English Gentleman* where William Bradbury was last seen alive © Bill Walden

Day had become a peripheral figure in the trial and was cleared of the charges. Even Worsley, who had been keen to implicate Welch in the hope of saving his own neck, indicated that Day was not responsible.

There was never much doubt that Worsley would be found guilty and sentenced to death. The newspapers reported that his execution attracted only a small crowd, but although public executions were falling out of fashion as a spectacle, one newspaper still numbered the crowd at approximately 4,000. Although there was to be a dribble of other public executions around the country, William Worsley was the last man to be executed in public in Bedfordshire.

Just a few months after he started his prison sentence Welch received a pardon. He returned to Luton before finally emigrating to start a new life overseas. The innocent James Day lived on in Luton and continued in his career as a straw hat manufacturer.

THE BLEDLOW RIDGE MURDER

JOHN KINGHAM LIVED AT NEWALLS FARM, CLOSE TO PRINCES RISBOROUGH. HE WAS LAST SEEN ALIVE ON THE EVENING OF 28TH SEPTEMBER 1893. WHEN THE NEIGHBOURS WERE ALERTED TO HIS UNCHARACTERISTIC DISAPPEARANCE, A PRELIMINARY SEARCH WAS CONDUCTED, ALTHOUGH WITHOUT ANY SUCCESS. THE NEXT MORNING THE SEARCH RESUMED AND KINGHAM'S BODY WAS LOCATED IN A NEARBY FIELD. ONE OF THE FIRST VISITORS TO THE SCENE OF THE CRIME WAS AN AGRICULTURAL LABOURER, JOHN AVERY, WHO IS TO FEATURE FURTHER AS THIS STORY OF AN UNSOLVED MURDER BEGINS TO UNFOLD.

As the first reports began to appear in the newspapers the story was simply that Kingham had heard a shot fired in the woods near to the farm and had gone to investigate, the belief being that he had surprised a gang of poachers. He had been beaten on the head and his throat cut. The blood-soaked ground showed no real sign of being disturbed, which suggested that Kingham had been given no time to fight for his life and that there had been little in the way of a struggle.

Kingham was a 57-year-old agricultural labourer and lived with his grandson, Herbert. On the night of the murder Herbert had gone out to play at about 5.30 leaving his grandfather cutting wood behind the house. Returning two hours later Herbert found the house empty and in darkness. He went to see a neighbour called George Martin to find out if he knew what was going on. George had last seen Kingham soon after 5 pm that evening and was as mystified as Herbert as to where he might be. A small number of locals, including the landlord of the pub, The Boot, now formed a gang to search the nearby woodland.

With the body discovered, the process of obtaining witness statements from those involved began. In providing his statement John Avery swiftly started to incriminate himself. Avery was 49 years old and came from Radnage, from a family of chairmakers, and he also worked as an agricultural labourer. He spoke of how he had heard voices in the woods and then later gunshots. At this stage, while admitting that he knew full well who the men involved were, he refused to name names. However, finding himself under arrest, he swiftly began to realise the seriousness of his situation and was soon prepared to name at least one of the people that he knew to be involved. Avery identified one of the voices as belonging to Jim Brooks, known locally as Patsy Brooks.

The Bledlow Ridge MURDER

The inquest into Kingham's death commenced at The Boot pub, two days after the murder. There was plenty of evidence to be heard but none of it really shed any light on why John Kingham might have been murdered. He was a quiet and well-liked man and he was certainly not wealthy. Although there was no certainty as to the number of assailants, there was always a belief that there were two men involved in the killing. With that possibility being considered Richard Avery, who was John's twin brother, was now arrested.

Traces of blood were found on the brothers' clothes and a witness was able to place Richard Avery on a path close to the scene of the crime and carrying a gun. In fact there was a wealth of evidence placing the Avery brothers around the periphery of the scene of the crime, but nothing to link them to the crime itself. Even the blood found on their clothes was found to be animal blood, just as Avery had predicted it would be, as they would often come into contact with animal blood in their everyday work. Nevertheless, despite the absence of any real evidence against them, the brothers were charged with murder and brought before the magistrates to decide whether they should stand trial.

Herbert, the grandson of the victim, was now able to recall an incident from the previous year. His grandfather had mentioned that, after testifying in a poaching case, he had received threats from the accused man: Patsy Brooks. At the inquest there was finally some evidence from Patsy Brooks himself. On the Thursday, the day of the murder, he said that he did not set foot in the woods at Yewsden, where Kingham was found. He stated that he had no quarrel with Kingham but, rather intriguingly, that the Brooks family and the Avery family were not friends.

Although Brooks had a watertight alibi, that was not the case with the Avery brothers who had been seen in the woods by a number of witnesses. The newspapers reported the particularly cool demeanour displayed by John Avery in particular throughout the entire episode. The feeling was that the case against Richard Avery was weak but that the case against John was reasonably strong, the trouble being that the evidence was only circumstantial. Additional doubt was cast over the involvement of either of them by the simple fact that Herbert reported that the Avery brothers were considered to be friends of his grandfather's and had absolutely no motive for murder.

So what did happen on that night in September 1893? Apparently Kingham's sister-in-law had an interesting story to tell, saying that she knew who was responsible and that it was 'two young chaps'. She declared her intention of telling the police, but that line of enquiry seems to have petered out. It seems possible that Brooks made sure that he had a perfectly good alibi for himself and then had the two brothers execute his revenge. But at that time the families were not friends and the alliance seems rather unlikely. On top of that, why would John Avery suddenly place Brooks as being in the woods close to the murder scene? There had been no necessity to do this unless it was an attack of conscience.

When the magistrates reported their conclusions it was decided that the brothers should not be tried for the murder of John Kingham and they were released. The fear was that if anyone was to stand trial and then be acquitted, then that would be the end of the charge against them and they would be unable to be tried a second time. **The murder remains unsolved.**

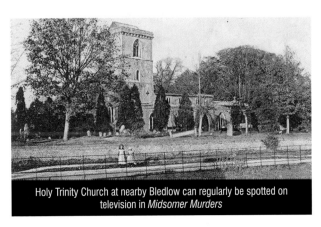

Holy Trinity Church at nearby Bledlow can regularly be spotted on television in *Midsomer Murders*

THE REDBOURN MURDER

DONALD LITTON WAS A BOY OF FOURTEEN YEARS OF AGE. HE RATHER FANCIED A TRIP TO THE ZOO AND, HAVING NO MONEY OF HIS OWN, DECIDED TO STEAL SOME FROM A NEIGHBOUR'S HOUSE. DONALD HAD DONE THIS BEFORE AND ON THOSE OCCASIONS HAD GAINED ADMISSION VIA AN UNLOCKED DOOR. ON THIS OCCASION, ALTHOUGH THE DOOR WAS NOW LOCKED, IT WAS STILL EASY ENOUGH TO GAIN ACCESS. HE COULD LITTLE REALISE, AS HE CLIMBED THROUGH THE WINDOW, THAT THIS ATTEMPT TO FUND HIS EXCURSION WOULD END IN MURDER.

In the weeks prior to the end of January 1921 the Seabrook family had noticed that money was going missing from their house at North Common in Redbourn. At one time a half crown seemed to have disappeared from the mantelpiece as well as a florin and twopence from a daughter's handbag. They were unable to explain the losses and, for the first time, they started to take the security of the house a little more seriously. They made sure that the doors were locked whenever they went out and left 71-year-old Sarah Seabrook alone in the house.

In the middle of the afternoon on 27th January a woman returned to the Seabrooks' house and found to her alarm that it was full of smoke. When she entered she found that a chair, which had a sheet over it for drying in front of the fire, had been pushed right up to the fireplace and was starting to burn. She threw out the sheet and opened the door to get rid of the smoke. When the smoke began to clear she heard a gurgling sound and then noticed Sarah Seabrook sitting on the floor with her back to the wall by the sink. At first she thought that she had had a stroke and ran for help. By coincidence her first port of call was the house of Mrs Litton. It was Donald Litton who answered the door in a state of undress, saying that his mother was not at home. Still desperate for assistance, the woman went to another neighbour where she was able to get help.

When the neighbours got back to Sarah's house they noticed that she was bleeding profusely from the head. They staunched the bleeding with sheets as best they could and Sarah was taken to Hemel Hempstead hospital where she died at 7.30 pm. During the initial police investigation Donald Litton's story was that he had fallen down a well at about two o'clock, and that was where he would have been at about the time of the murder. When police interrogated him they found his story extremely suspicious. Supposedly he had successfully negotiated a 17-foot climb with his back against one wall and his feet against the other. Donald claimed that this misadventure was the reason that he was undressed when the neighbours called as he had had to wash his clothes. Donald's statement was just one of a number taken in the early days of the case but after following some other lines of enquiry the police brought the boy back in for further questioning. It was then, six days after the murder, that Donald confessed to killing Sarah Seabrook.

In his statement Donald said he had gone to the house to steal money to go to the zoo but found the door bolted and so climbed in through a window. He had a hammer with him as he explored all the rooms, and when Sarah Seabrook had woken from her nap and seen him he had hit her a couple of times with the hammer and then fled.

He had already gone out and buried the hammer in the garden, but on returning to the house he found that Sarah was getting back up and so he hit her a few times more with the poker. Examination of Sarah showed that she had multiple wounds to the head and that her skull was fractured in eight places. In panic Donald claimed that he had decided to drown himself and so went to the well and climbed down. By the time that he got to the bottom he had changed his mind and managed to scramble back out. When the police went to the spot where he had buried the hammer they were able to dig it up and found that it had human hair on it. As further evidence they found that a plaster cast taken of the footprints in the mud around Sarah's house corresponded exactly with Donald's boots.

A fair proportion of Donald's trial concerned a slightly complicated point of law. Officially a child of fourteen was deemed incapable of committing a crime, such as the murder of Sarah, unless there was evidence of the prisoner having understanding and discretion in the matter. The sheer ferocity of the attack seemed to suggest that Donald was likely to be deemed responsible but Donald's defence contended that his responsibility was limited due to his age. In the end, Donald Litton was convicted of the murder of Sarah Seabrook and detained during His Majesty's pleasure.

North Common Redbourn © Nigel Cox

MYSTERY OF A SECRET

AT 31 YEARS OF AGE, ALBERT BODDY WAS A BRICKLAYER WITH A NUMBER OF CONVICTIONS FOR PETTY MISDEMEANOURS, OFTEN INVOLVING POACHING. BY MARCH 1937 HE WAS SPENDING A FAIR AMOUNT OF HIS TIME IN THE HOUR GLASS PUB IN HIGH WYCOMBE. IT WAS ON THE 27TH OF THAT MONTH THAT BODDY CAME INTO THE PUB AND SHOT DEAD KATHERINE GODBY.

Albert Boddy lived in Lane End Road, High Wycombe, where he shared a house with his married sister. The house was just a three or four-minute walk to the Hour Glass and it was from here that Albert had got to know Mrs Godby, with whom he frequently played darts and dominoes.

Katherine, along with her husband, Major Robert George Rhodes Godby, had lived in High Wycombe since the late 1920s. In 1921 he became a Flying Officer with the RAF but by the time of the events in this story he was back in civvy street. He married Katherine Comberbach in 1929. They had a home in High Wycombe but spent some time away travelling. At least part of this time was spent in New Zealand, where Robert had family connections; two of his sisters had even been born there. When they came back on a more permanent basis they lived in Mill End Road in Sands, High Wycombe.

A game of dominoes had been arranged for the evening of 27th March. After an afternoon poaching with a friend, George Allaway, Albert made his way to the Hour Glass where he met up with Katherine and some other friends of his. It seems that he became annoyed as Katherine failed to lavish all of her attention on him. There was no suggestion that Albert and Katherine were lovers but the prospect may well have been in Albert's mind. Although Boddy stayed for some hours, when he did leave it was in a huff.

Once away from the pub, Boddy attempted to borrow a gun. While this might normally ring alarm bells, Albert was well known for his poaching activities and so was soon able to get hold of a shotgun and four cartridges.

By the time that Albert was back in the pub it was nearly closing time and in the hubbub of activity a shot suddenly rang out. Boddy had shot Katherine in the head. A nearby policeman was called and as soon as he entered the Hour Glass Albert made it clear that he was handing himself in. Katherine was taken to the

War Memorial Hospital, but she was dead on arrival. Everyone was in agreement that Albert was fully sober at the time and in his statement he claimed that he loved Katherine and that the shooting was a spur-of-the-moment action after he had collected the gun to go poaching.

When it came to the trial, held in Aylesbury on 20th May 1937, Boddy's defence had become more convincing. He claimed that subsequent to the shooting his mind had gone blank and that he had no recollection of anything he said. Moreover, he claimed that he did not know that the gun was loaded and he was able to produce a witness to corroborate the story. Frederick Grey, from whom the gun had been borrowed, conceded the possibility that the gun may have been inadvertently left loaded as there was a precedent for this when he had accidentally left the unlicensed weapon loaded after returning from shooting some rabbits. Boddy's defence was that he thought the weapon was unloaded but that he still pointed it in the direction of Katherine in annoyance at the lack of attention that he was receiving from her. Indeed, there was evidence from the party at the table that night which suggested that Albert had spoken to Katherine but that she had ignored him.

A lot of time at the trial was spent considering the position of the gun. Had Boddy raised it to his shoulder or not? It was more plausible that the killing was an accident if the gun was not raised to the firing position. Yet the gun did seem to have been at shoulder height as Katherine was clearly and precisely picked out over the heads of the others sitting around the table.

The summing up of the evidence was meticulous and took ninety minutes. The jury took another forty minutes to find Boddy guilty of manslaughter and he was given a sentence of three years in gaol. The widower, Robert Godby, died in London in the 1950s but Albert survived into his eighties, still living in the Chilterns.

The Hour Glass, Sands, High Wycombe Google

THE LUTON SACK MURDER

WHEN HORACE MANTON, WHO WAS USUALLY KNOWN AS BERTIE, DIED IN PARKHURST PRISON ON THE ISLE OF WIGHT IN 1947 THE NEWS WENT ALMOST UNREPORTED. YET, JUST THREE YEARS EARLIER, HE HAD BEEN AT THE VERY CENTRE OF PROBABLY THE MOST NOTORIOUS MURDER STORY OF THIS REGION.

On 19th November 1943 a couple of workmen were walking along a river track when they happened to see a sack bobbing in the River Lea near the Vauxhall factory in Luton and were curious to know what it contained. Soon they were able to pull the sack from the river and on opening it were shocked to find that it contained the body of a woman. First appearances were that she had been beaten and strangled. The beating appeared to be so severe that identification of the victim was clearly going to be difficult.

The police were called and they conducted a thorough search of the area. Several sacks were eventually pulled from the river which also contained further remains of the same body. The body had only been in the river a few hours and yet the trail was already going cold. Photographs of the mysterious woman were shown at local cinemas without any immediate success. It was one of the first times in Britain that this approach was used, but even so they were unable to trace the victim. One of the sacks bore the name of Frank Redman, but this evidence did little to advance the case. Nor was there much to be gleaned from the body itself. One of the few clues was that there were marks to be seen on her middle finger which seemed to suggest to some that she might have been a heavy munitions worker.

The police investigation was meticulous. The cinema appeal had led to the tracing of some 500 missing women, each having to be followed up, but the identity of the victim still remained a mystery. Refuse tips were now searched and each scrap of clothing recovered was tested for any traces of blood. It was slow going and it took a further three months for the police to get a lead. In February 1944 police were again searching through household waste on a local tip, when a dog was spotted playing with a piece of material. Purely on a hunch, this clue was investigated further and the fabric turned out to be a piece of a woman's coat that had a dry-cleaning tag on it. The mark was traced to a Mrs Caroline Manton, who was found to have handed the coat in at the dry cleaners in the previous November.

It was at this stage that the police first spoke to Mrs Manton's husband, Horace – or Bertie – who was a 40-year-old fire brigade driver living in Regent Street. Bertie flatly denied that the photos of the body were of Caroline and told the officers that she was not at home simply because she had left him to live with her brother in London. In corroboration of his story he was even able to produce letters which he claimed had been written by Caroline in the period since she had moved away. The police were suspicious of both the cover story and of the letters themselves. They noted that the letters referred to the area of north London where she had gone as 'Hamstead'. The police asked Bertie for a sample of his own handwriting and he promptly incriminated himself by misspelling the same word.

With Bertie very much in the frame for the murder, the police conducted a thorough search of the Manton household. Throughout the entirety of the house they managed to locate only a single fingerprint belonging to Caroline. This was found on an old jar of pickle. This level of cleanliness as far as the fingerprints were concerned aroused suspicion. It seemed highly unlikely that in a house that had been Caroline's home for some years there should be so few signs of her having ever been there.

Bertie was arrested and charged with the murder of his wife. Realising that his situation was now hopeless he confessed to killing Caroline. Mrs Manton was five years younger than Bertie and he had married her when she was just 18 years of age. Lately he said that she had been 'keeping bad company' and smoking and drinking too much. He admitted that in the heat of a bitter argument he had hit her with a stool. In a desperate attempt to get rid of the body he had then wheeled Caroline's remains to the river on his bicycle. As a child Bertie had lived close to the river in Park Street and it was near here that he had attempted to submerge the sacks in the water. Manton appeared for trial at Bedford Assizes, where he was found guilty and sentenced to death, although this sentence was subsequently commuted to life imprisonment.

Bertie Manton
© Bill Walden

TERRIBLE TRAGEDY AT LITTLE KIMBLE

IN AUGUST 1914, JUST A COUPLE OF WEEKS AFTER GREAT BRITAIN ENTERED THE FIRST WORLD WAR, THE POLICE WERE CALLED TO A SHED SITUATED CLOSE TO LITTLE KIMBLE RAILWAY STATION. HERE THEY FOUND THE BODIES OF TWO MEN, CHARLES BUSBY AND WALTER TUCKER. BOTH MEN HAD BEEN EMPLOYED AS PLATELAYERS ON THE RAILWAY AND BOTH OF THEM HAD BEEN BATTERED TO DEATH.

Thomas Gilbert lived at 3 Icknield Cottages, Little Kimble, just off the Ellesborough Road close to the station. He was a 45-year-old employee of the railways, and was in charge of a small team of platelayers. Gilbert was married and had three children. In work he had the reputation of being very difficult and had even been moved within the company for that very reason.

Gilbert's team consisted of Charles Busby, aged 29, of Thame Road, Princes Risborough and Walter Tucker, aged 26, of Owlswick. Previously, in fact right up until the week of the murder, there had been a fourth member of the team called Albert Stone who was working with the others on the stretch of track close to Little Kimble leading to Marsh crossing.

Gilbert felt that Stone had become the victim of some childish pranks which were being carried out behind his back by the rest of the team. As his supervisor, Gilbert felt that it was his duty to let Stone know, and this was something which he immediately did. The others claimed that Gilbert was lying and, with all the animosity now out in the open, it was Busby who took the matter to the hierarchy in the railways, claiming that he was being bullied. A formal hearing was now arranged at Great Kimble railway station on 28th August in the hope of clearing the air.

The hearing was pretty acrimonious, with Gilbert reiterating his claims and also adding for good measure that Tucker was always spoiling for a fight and never happy to accept any instructions. Conversely, Busby reported that Gilbert's behaviour was extremely odd and verged on paranoia with him constantly believing that the others were plotting his downfall.

Early on the morning after the meeting Gilbert was spotted by his next-door neighbour, who coincidentally was the stationmaster, on his way to work. The stationmaster reported that Gilbert seemed his usual self and not distracted in any way. However, it was just a short while later, at 7.15, that Gilbert turned up at the house of a local police officer confessing to a double murder. The police were taken to the tool shed, which was a small cabin of no more than 13 feet by 9 feet, and it was here that the bodies of Busby and Tucker were found along with a bloody pickaxe handle.

Just prior to this incident there had been an attack on a signalman at Northchurch near Berkhamsted, about fifteen miles away, and it was at first rumoured that this incident was in some way related to the Little Kimble murders. Although Gilbert was already in custody only later did it become clear to the public that the killer came from far closer to home than many had realised.

At the inquest into the killings, which was held at the Crown Inn in Little Kimble, the tide of opinion was unsurprisingly very much against Gilbert. His reputation as a strict and peculiar supervisor was reinforced and he seemed to have little to say in the way of mitigating circumstances. He reported that Busby had spoken about getting hold of a revolver with which he intended to kill him. In response to this supposed threat, he had knocked both men to the ground using the pickaxe handle. Gilbert was now taken to Oxford Prison to await trial for the murder.

Little Kimble Station © Des Blenkinsopp

The trial was held in Aylesbury and Gilbert's plea was that of insanity, as he admitted just about all of the accusations against him. It was here that for the first time the testimony of Albert Stone, the fourth member of the plate-laying team, was heard and he did nothing to dispel the portrait of Gilbert as an extremely difficult work colleague. Stone was asked whether he believed that the two dead men had been good workmen and of a good character and he readily confirmed that they were. There was further evidence produced of Gilbert believing that he was being victimised and at one point he even claimed that he was being poisoned by the men working under him. Indeed the supposed 'poison' had been sent away for analysis but was found to be harmless.

When the jury were left to consider the evidence it took them just fifteen minutes to return the verdict of guilty. Although sentenced to death, an appeal duly followed and it was decided that Gilbert was insane at the time that he committed the murders. He was detained at His Majesty's pleasure.

Thomas Gilbert died at the age of 69 in 1938.

MURDER AT WATLINGTON

THE WATLINGTON MURDER CASE IS ONE THAT HAS MANY SIMILARITIES WITH THAT OF THE DUNSTABLE MURDER CASE INVOLVING DAVID DUMPLETON, WHICH APPEARS ELSEWHERE IN THIS BOOK. ALTHOUGH MANY WOULD SAY THAT THERE IS LITTLE DOUBT AS TO THE IDENTITY OF THE MURDERER, THE TRIAL FOR THE WATLINGTON MURDER DELIVERED A VERY DIFFERENT VERDICT.

At 11 pm on 25th September 1850 John Lambourn, aged 54, went to get help from neighbours saying that his wife was lying dead in the garden. The two neighbours accompanied John back to his house where they were to find John's wife, Ann, mortally wounded. She was just outside the door to the house and seemed to have received a severe blow to the back of the head.

The doctor was summoned and Ann, who apparently had never enjoyed the best of health, was taken to the bedroom where she died in the early part of the next morning from the effects of what in fact were a series of head wounds. The injuries had probably been caused by a set of fire tongs which were bloodstained and found placed prominently by the Lambourns' fireplace. As Ann had been hit from behind, and there was a trail of blood to be found in the garden, it was deduced that she had spent some time trying to flee from her assailant.

By the following afternoon John was starting to get his facts in order. He claimed that he had returned home and found the house in darkness. As he went in, he heard a gurgling sound which he then realised was Ann, and at that point he rushed out to get help from the neighbours. The facts did not entirely support this account as he would have been unable to enter the house without stepping over Ann's body. Nevertheless he now claimed to be wholly innocent.

The inquest, held at the Hare and Hounds in Watlington, heard about the tempestuous relationship the Lambourns had and of the abusive way that John behaved towards his wife. While they had no children or lodgers to give evidence regarding the constant quarrels, the nearest neighbours, the Coles family, did testify to the constant bickering between the Lambourns. It seems that the quarrel on the night of the murder concerned the lacklustre way in which Ann was making John's tea. Other witnesses related that John was known to boast about how one day he would kill Ann. On the night in question there were witnesses to a particularly ferocious quarrel which involved John storming out to go down to the pub for an hour. Things looked bleak for Lambourn, who was now taken to Oxford Castle to await trial for the murder of Ann.

Despite the wealth of testimony against John, he steadfastly maintained his innocence. The sum total of his alibi was that he claimed to have been out on the night in question; not that he was able to produce anybody to corroborate this. Certainly at the time of the inquest and trial there was little doubt in the minds of many people that John was responsible. The house contained little of value worth stealing. If it was an attempted robbery that had gone wrong then this unknown robber would have to have beaten and chased Ann and then, having murdered her, stolen nothing and carefully replaced the fire tongs having not thought to bring a weapon of his own. No other suspect was in the frame for the murder and yet after a trial of six hours' duration and an hour of deliberation a verdict of not guilty was returned by the jury.

THE WOODCOTE MURDER

FANNY PHILLIPS WAS A WIDOW, NOW IN HER EIGHTIES AND LIVING ALONE IN WOODCOTE FOLLOWING THE DEATH OF HER HUSBAND FIVE YEARS PREVIOUSLY. ON 8TH MAY 1839 A FRIEND WHO LIVED LOCALLY SPOTTED THAT THE DOOR HAD BEEN FORCED ON MRS PHILLIPS' HOUSE. ACCOMPANIED BY HER HUSBAND SHE CAME TO INVESTIGATE, ONLY TO FIND THAT HER FRIEND HAD BEEN MURDERED IN HER BED.

Mrs Phillips had been beaten terribly around the head. It was clear that the motive was robbery as the place was ransacked and a ring had even been torn from the finger of the dead woman. The intruder had long gone, but he had left behind the tools that he had used to gain admittance into the locked house. The tools were quickly identified as belonging to another local resident, a man called John Hore, although he was clearly innocent of the crime, having lost the tools in an earlier robbery.

As the police began to investigate, it was James Lambden, the husband of Mrs Phillips' friend who had earlier discovered the body, who was able to produce the vital clue. He remembered a farmworker, a man called Charles Morley, taking a particular interest in Mrs Phillips. Morley was a man in his early thirties and had been working as a casual labourer on the local farms and had once been heard wondering, in public, if she might have some money stashed away around the house. Shortly after the crime it was noted by others that Morley appeared to be considerably better off than he had been of late as he splashed his money around in all the local pubs.

Having been taken in for a police interview, Morley was able to stand up to the questioning without letting anything incriminating slip. However, a search of his house did reveal a file which belonged with the other tools left at the murder scene. Despite this, Morley still brazened it out, saying that he had simply found the file lying by the side of the road. Morley maintained his innocence and the police struggled to find any concrete evidence, in the end settling for charging him with the theft of the tools.

Morley obviously considered himself to have got off pretty lightly and was soon boasting to fellow prisoners, as he awaited trial for the theft of the tools, that he had got away with murder and also a considerable sum of money which he had stashed away. Soon Morley was tried for the theft charges, found guilty and, because of his long-standing criminal record, he actually received a sentence of transportation to Australia. The impending deportation was not the only impediment to his plan of returning to collect the proceeds of the murder. Morley's bragging now backfired when one of the prisoners he was with in Oxford Gaol, a man called Blackall who was awaiting trial for sheep stealing, was acquitted of the charges that he was facing and promptly chose to tell the authorities about Morley's confession.

Piecing together the story from the evidence at the scene of the crime and from Morley's boasts, it was now known that Mrs Phillips had woken up in the middle of the robbery. Morley had killed her and made off with upwards of £300 which was now stashed away in the roof of his house. With the money safely recovered the situation was bleak for the surprisingly upbeat Morley who, with a strange misunderstanding of the laws of double jeopardy, fully expected to be spared the gallows. Morley apparently believed that he would escape the death penalty on the grounds that he had already been convicted of stealing the tools and was about to be sent to New South Wales to serve his term of seven years' transportation. In fact he was taken from his confinement on a prison hulk in Woolwich straight back to court to be tried for murder.

The Woodcote MURDER

Charles Morley was tried in Oxford on 2nd March 1840. The jury retired for just ten minutes before returning a verdict of guilty. Throughout he insisted he was innocent and continued to protest his innocence right up to his execution at Oxford Gaol three weeks later.

Oxford Prison where Morley was executed The Author

THE SANDRIDGE MURDER

AT 3 AM ON 22ND AUGUST 1880 AT A FARM SITUATED IN SANDRIDGE, CLOSE TO ST ALBANS, 68-YEAR-OLD FARMER EDWARD ANSTEE WAS WOKEN BY THE SOUND OF AN INTRUDER OUTSIDE. OPENING THE WINDOW TO SEE WHAT WAS HAPPENING, EDWARD WAS PROMPTLY SHOT IN THE FACE AT POINT-BLANK RANGE.

The farm was a comparatively modest four-bedroomed house in what was then a remote position. It was situated roughly where The Quadrant now is in Marshal's Drive. On the night in question a young servant called Elizabeth Coleman was also staying at the house. She was sleeping in the attic when she was awoken by two gunshots. She didn't see anything outside but could now hear the intruder inside the house looking for valuables.

The intruder was soon to blunder into the bedroom of another servant, Susan Lindsay, where he demanded to know where the money was kept. Susan said that she did not know, and when she started to scream for help the intruder left the room again in order to continue his search for the loot. Soon he was back at

Susan's door, yelling through the keyhole for her to give him some clue as to where the money was kept. With Susan maintaining that she knew nothing about the money the intruder swiftly lowered his sights. He now said that he would be prepared to accept a payment of five shillings in return for him and his two accomplices not battering down the door and beating her up. After further negotiation he said that he would accept two shillings. After Susan pushed the money under the door the intruder stomped off back downstairs to continue ransacking the house.

Before long the burglar could be seen from the windows of the farm leaving with some items tucked underneath his arm. Fortunately at this stage Susan did not unlock the door as he was back within ten minutes for a second and final load.

A further 45 minutes were to pass before Susan risked unlocking the door to see the damage. It was not long before she was united with Elizabeth and discovering the body of Mr Anstee. He had been shot in the face by the intruder who had been standing on a ladder stolen from a nearby hayrick. It was by now around the time when work would normally be starting at the farm and, looking out of the window, Elizabeth saw one of the workers on his way to the farmyard. Back inside the house the three of them took stock of the situation. The ladder and some tools had been left outside Mr Anstee's window and some silver items seemed to have been taken. Now the police in St. Albans were summoned to the house.

Susan related that by the time that the intruder appeared at her door he was using an oil lamp and so she had the chance to get a reasonable look at him. She described him as short and in his mid-forties and with greying hair and a moustache. More distinctive than his physical appearance was his voice, which Susan described as peculiar.

To the police it had already seemed that this was the latest in a sequence of robberies at remote farms. They already had a suspect in mind and an arrest was made that very evening at the Pineapple public house in Catherine Street, St. Albans. The man in question was 42-year-old Thomas Wheeler and at this stage he was arrested for one of the earlier robberies which had been at the farm of a Mr Jacob Reynolds back in June. However, even at this stage, it was very much in their minds to also charge him for the more serious crime committed at Mr Anstee's farm.

Wheeler had spent his formative years in St. Albans but previously had lived in South London. He was a heavy-drinking womaniser who had left his wife and children for a life of crime and wandering. Earlier in the year of the murder, he had spent time back in south London as an inmate of Wandsworth Prison. On release from his five-month sentence for robbery he was soon back in the Chilterns area and desperate for money. He had carried out at least one other burglary, which was very similar in nature to the one at Anstee's farm, and had attempted to hide the stolen goods from that crime at his brother's house.

Clearly finding a hiding place for the stolen property from the sequence of robberies was proving the most difficult part for Wheeler. The items taken from Marshals Wick (the Anstee farm) were recovered from a wheat field at the same time as a gun that had been used in both the earlier robbery and for killing Mr Anstee. Clothing was also recovered which was identified as belonging to Wheeler, and with him being so clearly linked to the robberies the case against him became cast iron. Wheeler's initial alibi was that he could not have committed the murder as he was in St. Thomas's Hospital at the time, a point that he attempted to prove by adopting an extravagant limp.

Thomas Wheeler was tried at Chelmsford with the case commencing on 2nd November 1880. There was overwhelming evidence against the defendant and a picture emerged of his clueless bumbling around the vicinity of the crime scene in the hours before and after the murder. He was seen in the pubs trying to borrow money and later using what was surely the stolen florin taken from Susan to buy drinks. Later he was spotted carrying a gun, and yet again he was seen walking up the railway track towards Harpenden where he was spotted by a couple of signalmen and told to get off the line. He had no sensible alibi and had even dispensed with the limp. His voice, which Sarah in particular had recalled as being so unusual, was also there for all to hear. The newspapers recorded how he spoke rapidly and with 'indistinct utterance'.

While Wheeler's defence was that all of the evidence was purely circumstantial, there was never much doubt that he would be found guilty. It took the jury twenty-four minutes to return their verdict.

At first Wheeler spent his time in St. Albans Gaol asserting his innocence before eventually realising that the game really was up and that it was time to confess to the murder. **When hanged on 29th November 1880 Wheeler became the first person to be executed at the St. Albans prison.**